STEVE JO

SADDLEBACK
EDUCATIONAL PUBLISHING

Saddleback's Graphic Biographies

SADDLEBACK
EDUCATIONAL PUBLISHING
www.sdlback.com

ISBN-13: 978-1-61651-889-9
ISBN-10: 1-61651-889-8
eBook: 978-1-61247-623-0

Printed in Guangzhou, China
0312/CA21200403

16 15 14 13 12 1 2 3 4 5

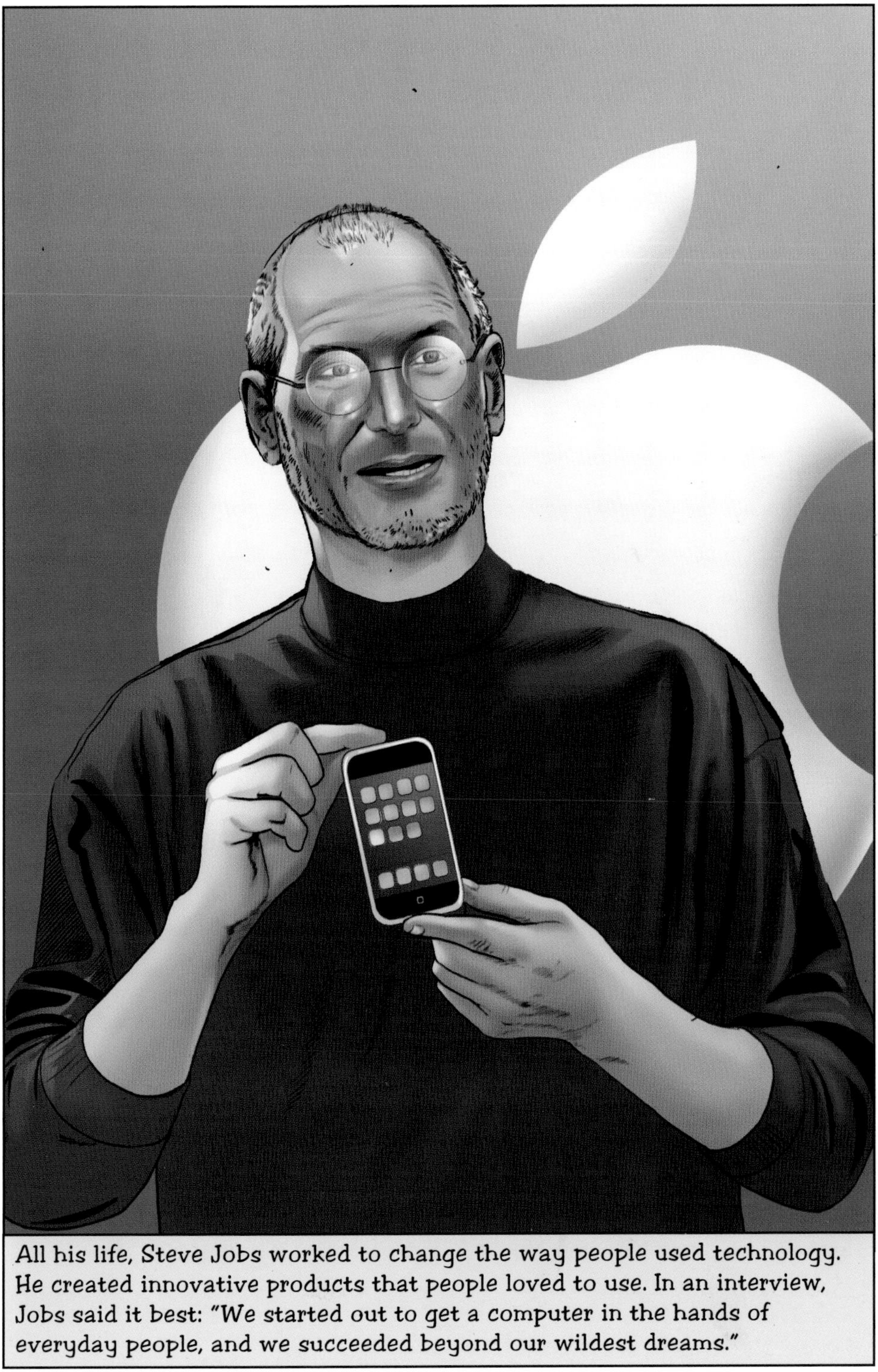

All his life, Steve Jobs worked to change the way people used technology. He created innovative products that people loved to use. In an interview, Jobs said it best: "We started out to get a computer in the hands of everyday people, and we succeeded beyond our wildest dreams."

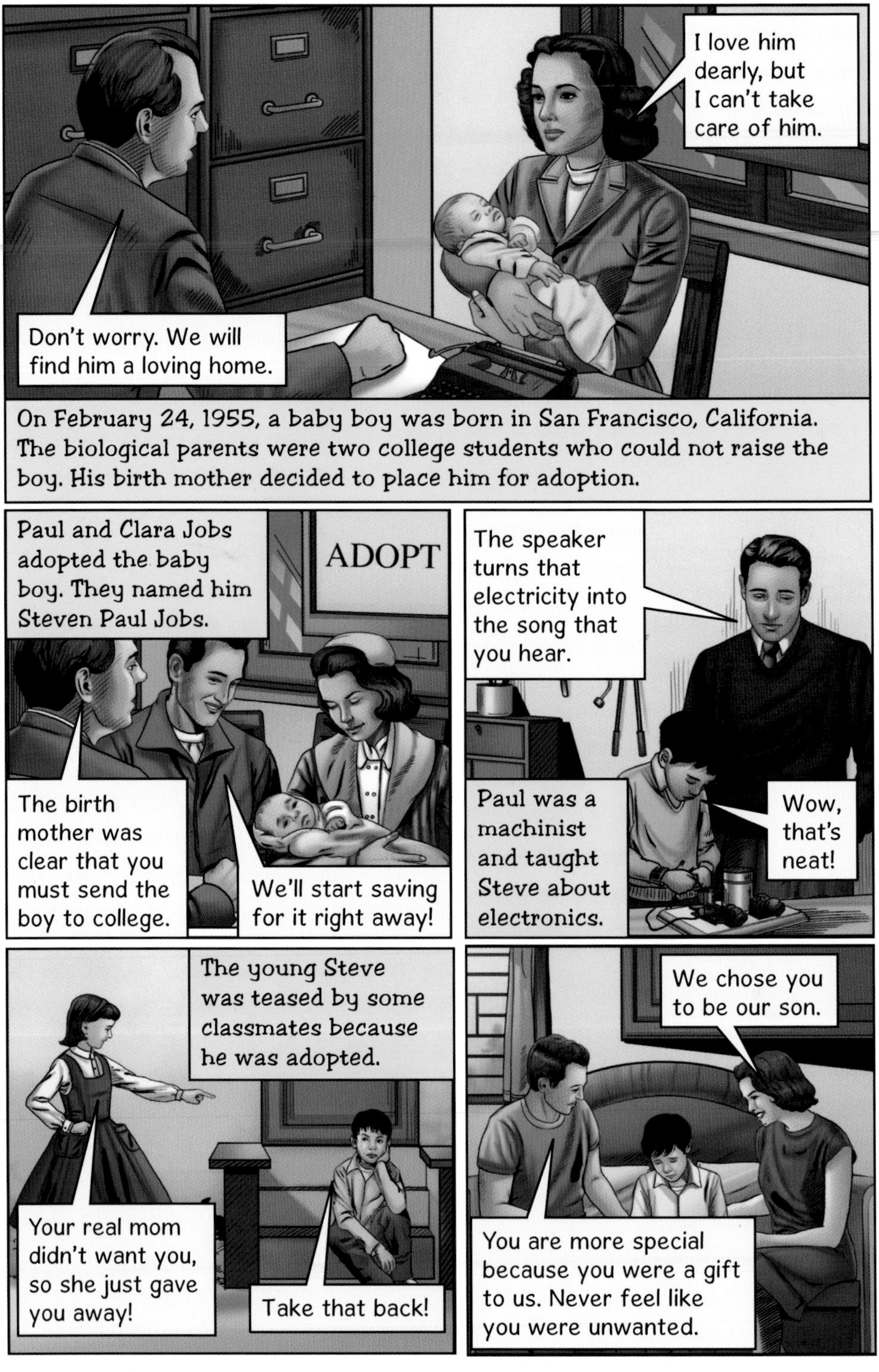
I love him dearly, but I can't take care of him.
Don't worry. We will find him a loving home.
On February 24, 1955, a baby boy was born in San Francisco, California. The biological parents were two college students who could not raise the boy. His birth mother decided to place him for adoption.
Paul and Clara Jobs adopted the baby boy. They named him Steven Paul Jobs.
ADOPT
The birth mother was clear that you must send the boy to college.
We'll start saving for it right away!
The speaker turns that electricity into the song that you hear.
Paul was a machinist and taught Steve about electronics.
Wow, that's neat!
The young Steve was teased by some classmates because he was adopted.
Your real mom didn't want you, so she just gave you away!
Take that back!
We chose you to be our son.
You are more special because you were a gift to us. Never feel like you were unwanted.

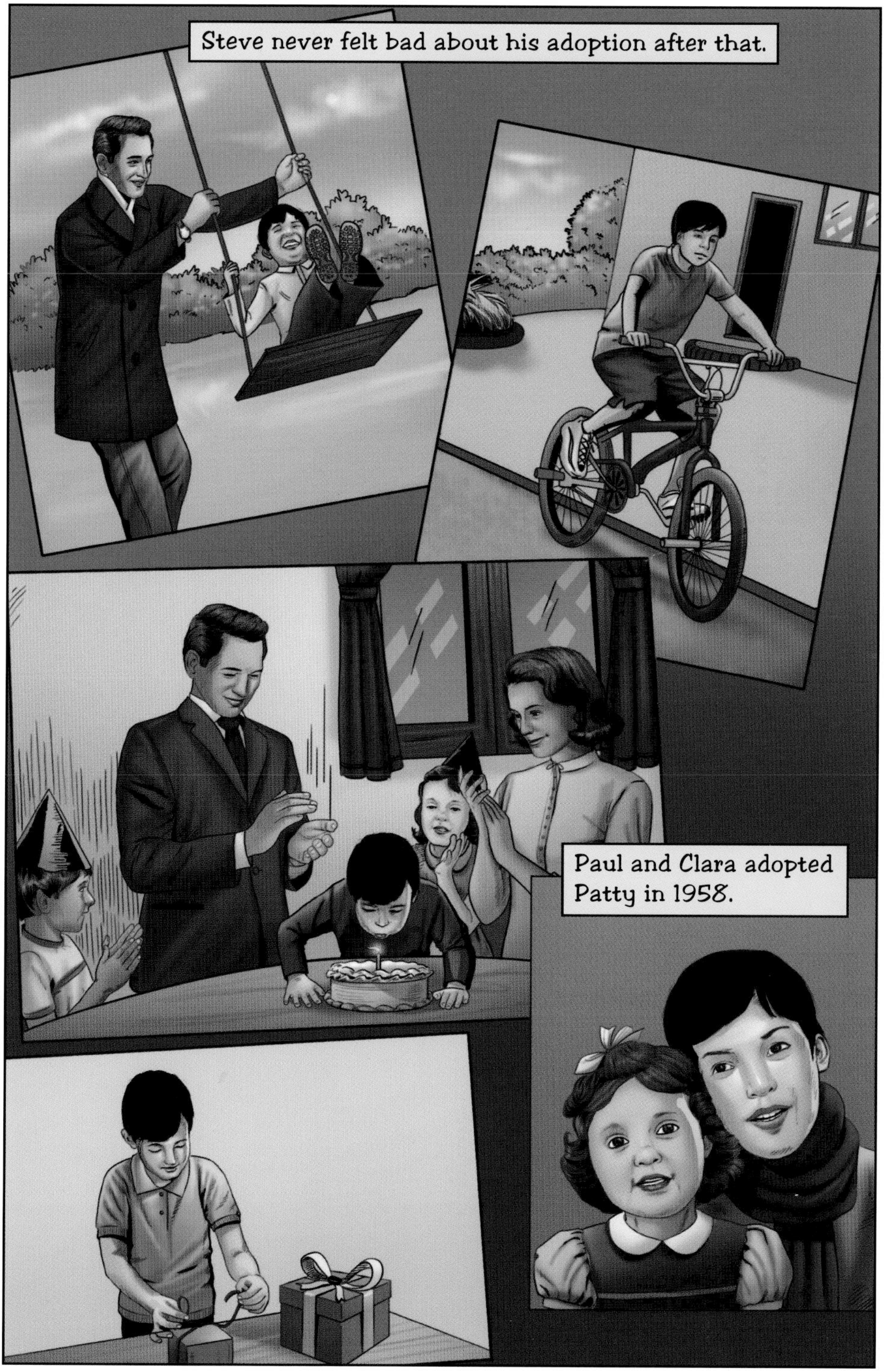
Steve never felt bad about his adoption after that.
Paul and Clara adopted Patty in 1958.

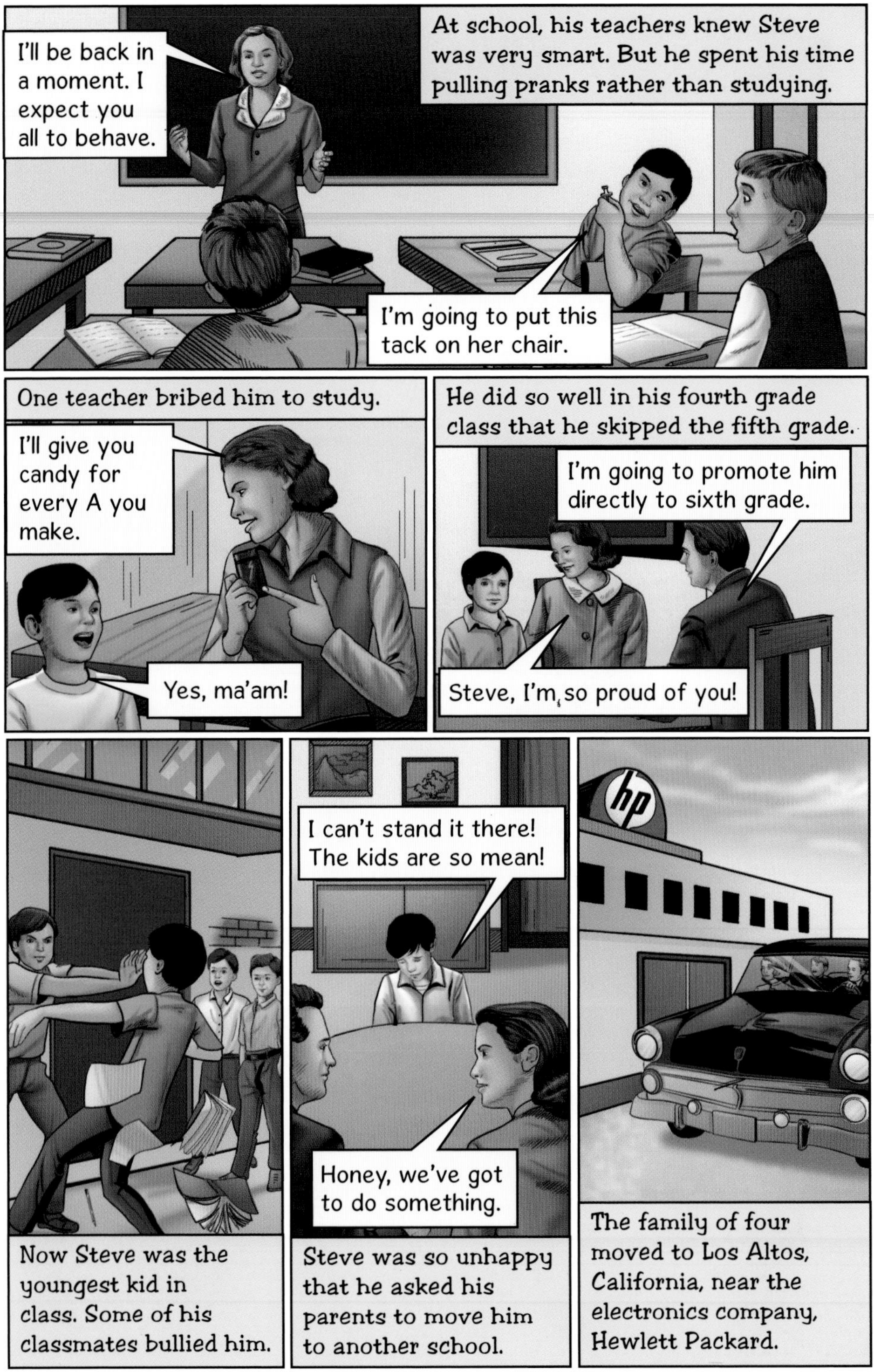
At school, his teachers knew Steve was very smart. But he spent his time pulling pranks rather than studying.
I'll be back in a moment. I expect you all to behave.
I'm going to put this tack on her chair.
One teacher bribed him to study.
I'll give you candy for every A you make.
Yes, ma'am!
He did so well in his fourth grade class that he skipped the fifth grade.
I'm going to promote him directly to sixth grade.
Steve, I'm so proud of you!
Now Steve was the youngest kid in class. Some of his classmates bullied him.
I can't stand it there! The kids are so mean!
Honey, we've got to do something.
Steve was so unhappy that he asked his parents to move him to another school.
hp
The family of four moved to Los Altos, California, near the electronics company, Hewlett Packard.

In high school, Steve met someone who would have a big impact on his life. He met college student Steve Wozniak. Everybody called him Woz.

Hey! What's wrong with the TV?!?

The two Steves quickly became friends. They both loved playing with electronics. Sometimes they would get into trouble with a TV-jamming machine they invented.

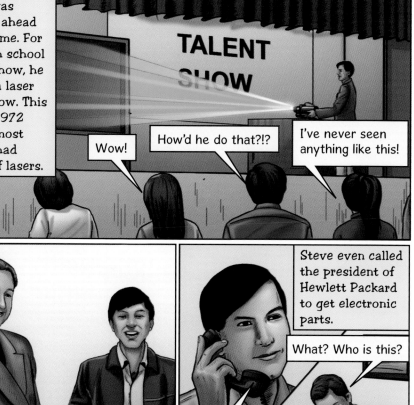

Steve was already ahead of his time. For the high school talent show, he put on a laser light show. This was in 1972 before most people had heard of lasers.

TALENT SHOW

Wow!

How'd he do that?!?

I've never seen anything like this!

He loved attending his electronics class.

Steve even called the president of Hewlett Packard to get electronic parts.

What? Who is this?

Does HP have some spare parts they can send to me?

President

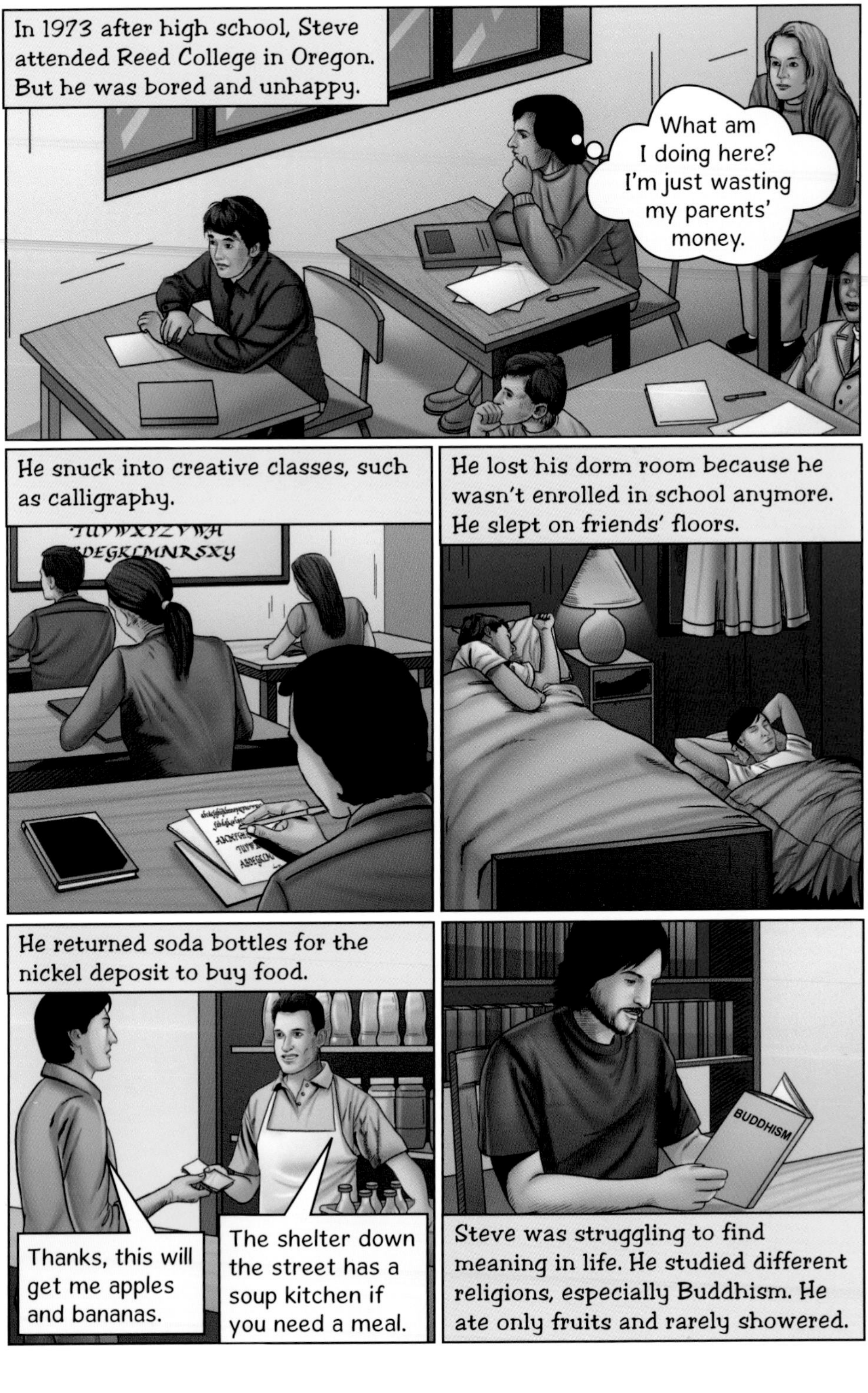
In 1973 after high school, Steve attended Reed College in Oregon. But he was bored and unhappy.
What am I doing here? I'm just wasting my parents' money.
He snuck into creative classes, such as calligraphy.
He lost his dorm room because he wasn't enrolled in school anymore. He slept on friends' floors.
He returned soda bottles for the nickel deposit to buy food.
Thanks, this will get me apples and bananas.
The shelter down the street has a soup kitchen if you need a meal.
BUDDHISM
Steve was struggling to find meaning in life. He studied different religions, especially Buddhism. He ate only fruits and rarely showered.

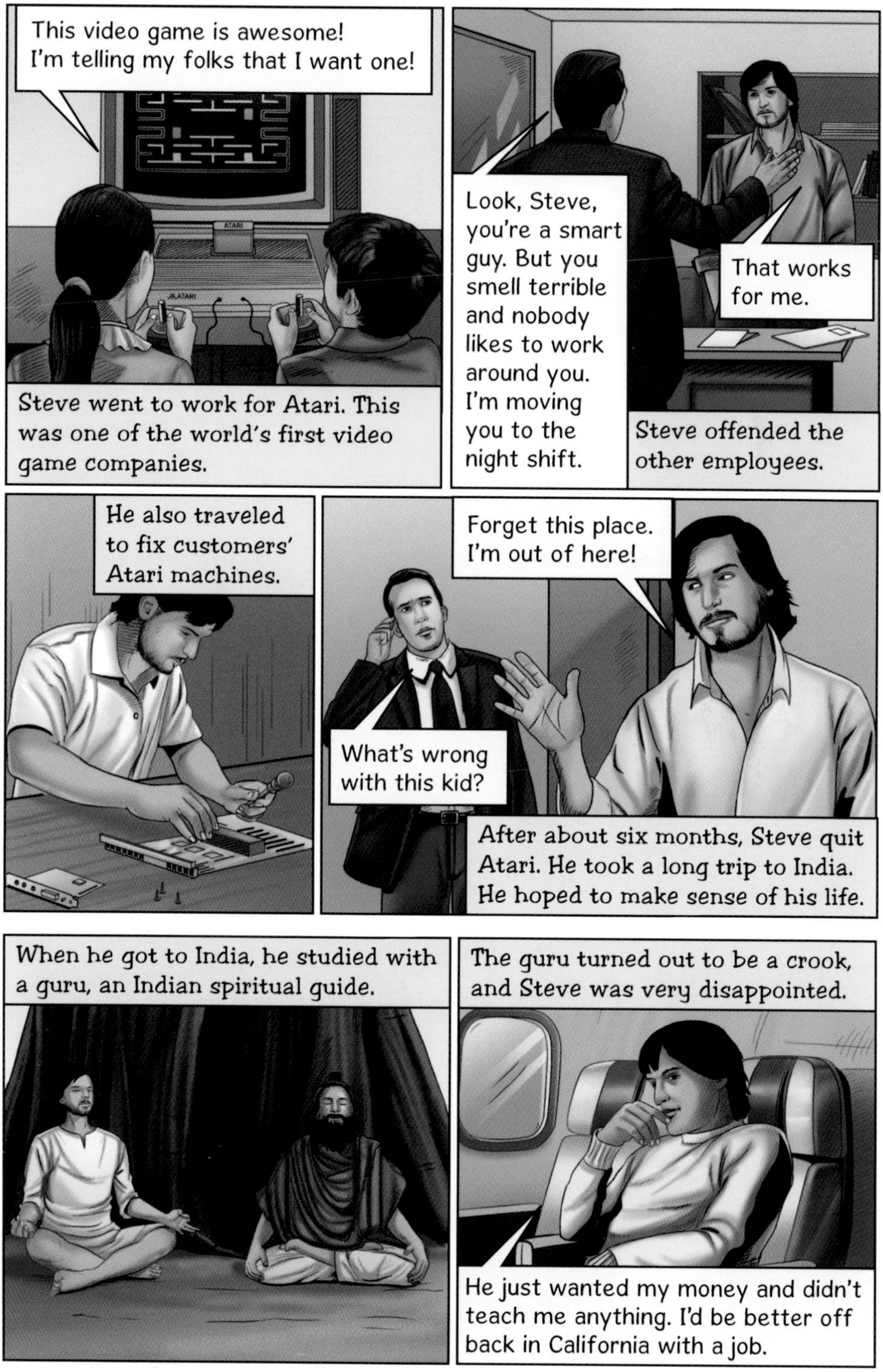
This video game is awesome! I'm telling my folks that I want one!
ATARI
ATARI
Steve went to work for Atari. This was one of the world's first video game companies.
Look, Steve, you're a smart guy. But you smell terrible and nobody likes to work around you. I'm moving you to the night shift.
That works for me.
Steve offended the other employees.
He also traveled to fix customers' Atari machines.
Forget this place. I'm out of here!
What's wrong with this kid?
After about six months, Steve quit Atari. He took a long trip to India. He hoped to make sense of his life.
When he got to India, he studied with a guru, an Indian spiritual guide.
The guru turned out to be a crook, and Steve was very disappointed.
He just wanted my money and didn't teach me anything. I'd be better off back in California with a job.

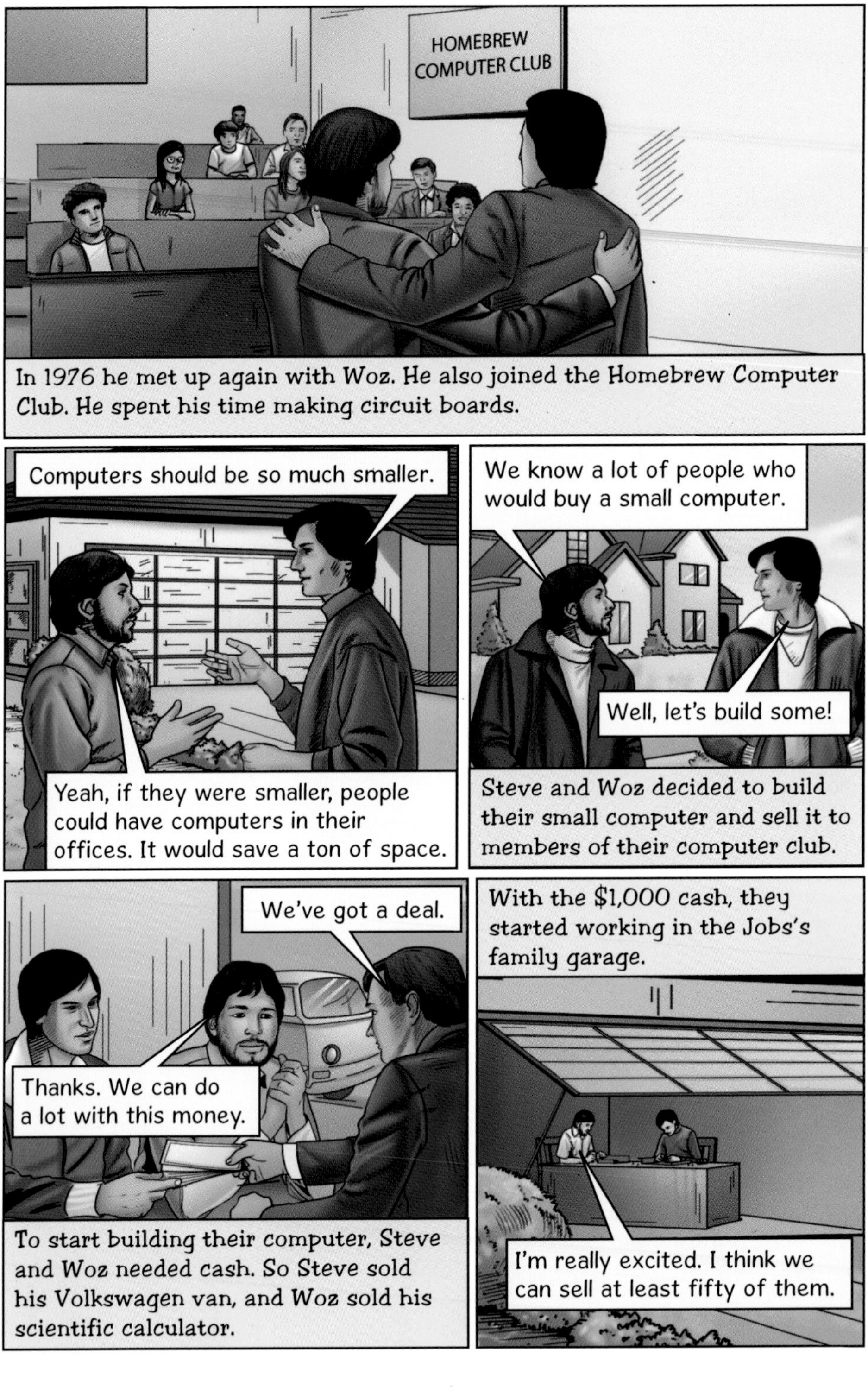
HOMEBREW COMPUTER CLUB
In 1976 he met up again with Woz. He also joined the Homebrew Computer Club. He spent his time making circuit boards.
Computers should be so much smaller.
Yeah, if they were smaller, people could have computers in their offices. It would save a ton of space.
We know a lot of people who would buy a small computer.
Well, let's build some!
Steve and Woz decided to build their small computer and sell it to members of their computer club.
We've got a deal.
Thanks. We can do a lot with this money.
To start building their computer, Steve and Woz needed cash. So Steve sold his Volkswagen van, and Woz sold his scientific calculator.
With the $1,000 cash, they started working in the Jobs's family garage.
I'm really excited. I think we can sell at least fifty of them.

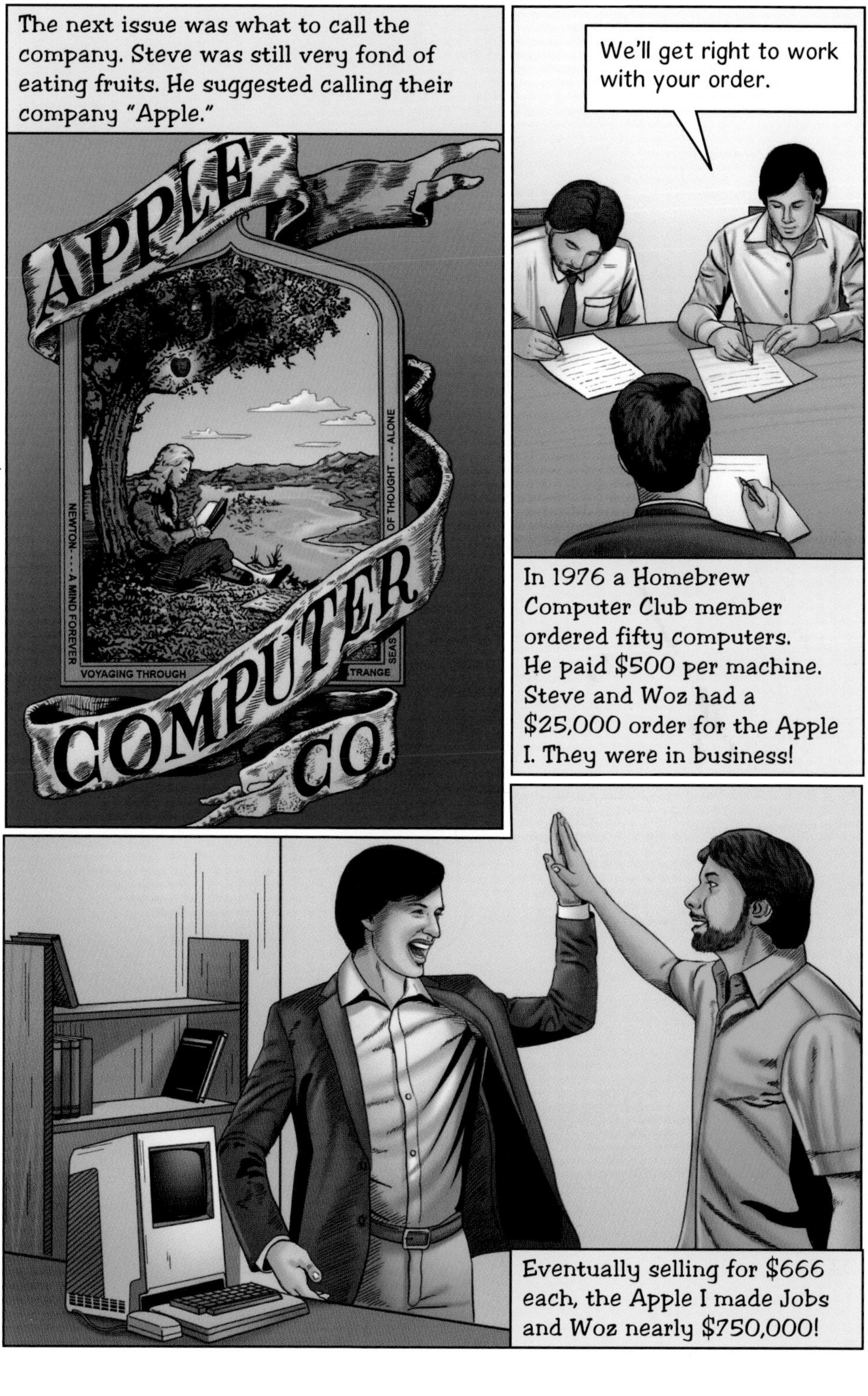
The next issue was what to call the company. Steve was still very fond of eating fruits. He suggested calling their company "Apple."
APPLE COMPUTER CO.
NEWTON . . . A MIND FOREVER VOYAGING THROUGH
TRANGE SEAS OF THOUGHT . . . ALONE
We'll get right to work with your order.
In 1976 a Homebrew Computer Club member ordered fifty computers. He paid $500 per machine. Steve and Woz had a $25,000 order for the Apple I. They were in business!
Eventually selling for $666 each, the Apple I made Jobs and Woz nearly $750,000!

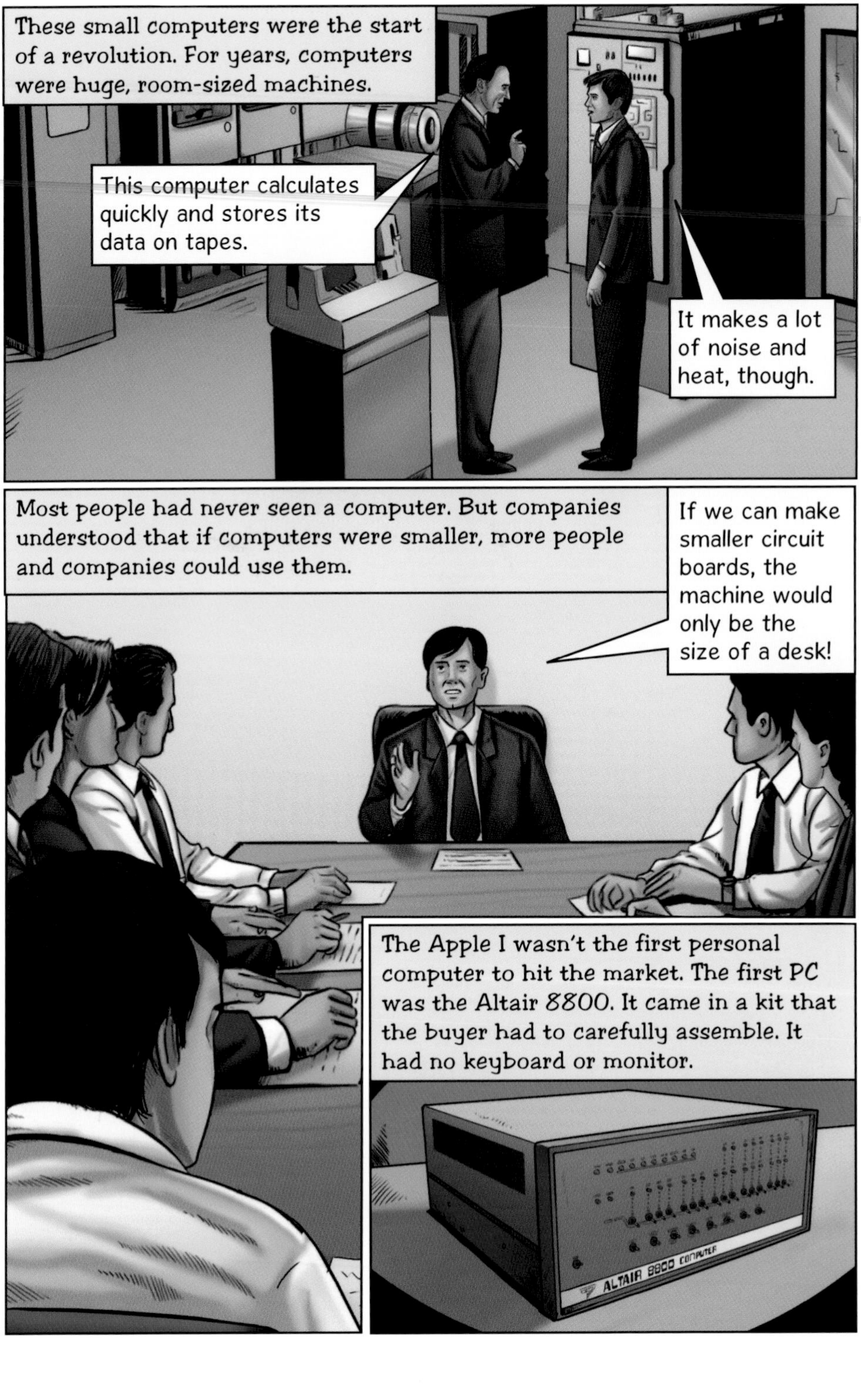
These small computers were the start of a revolution. For years, computers were huge, room-sized machines.
This computer calculates quickly and stores its data on tapes.
It makes a lot of noise and heat, though.
Most people had never seen a computer. But companies understood that if computers were smaller, more people and companies could use them.
If we can make smaller circuit boards, the machine would only be the size of a desk!
The Apple I wasn't the first personal computer to hit the market. The first PC was the Altair 8800. It came in a kit that the buyer had to carefully assemble. It had no keyboard or monitor.
ALTAIR 8800 COMPUTER

IBM had been in business since the 1920s, making business machines. IBM was a major computer manufacturer when Apple was just beginning.

We just got a contract to make computers for NASA.

IBM was racing to make small computers like most other computer companies in the 1970s.

Our new computer only weighs fifty-five pounds! Notice it has a nice five-inch monitor and a built-in keyboard.

How much does it cost?

The basic version is just $11,000. If you want all the bells and whistles, it's $24,000.

Steve and Woz understood that personal computers had to be both small and affordable.

Incredible! I can buy sixteen of your Apples for less than the cost of one IBM!

A bigger monitor would be much easier to read.

But because their startup was so successful, Steve and Woz were already looking ahead.

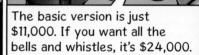

And the circuits should calculate and process data much faster.

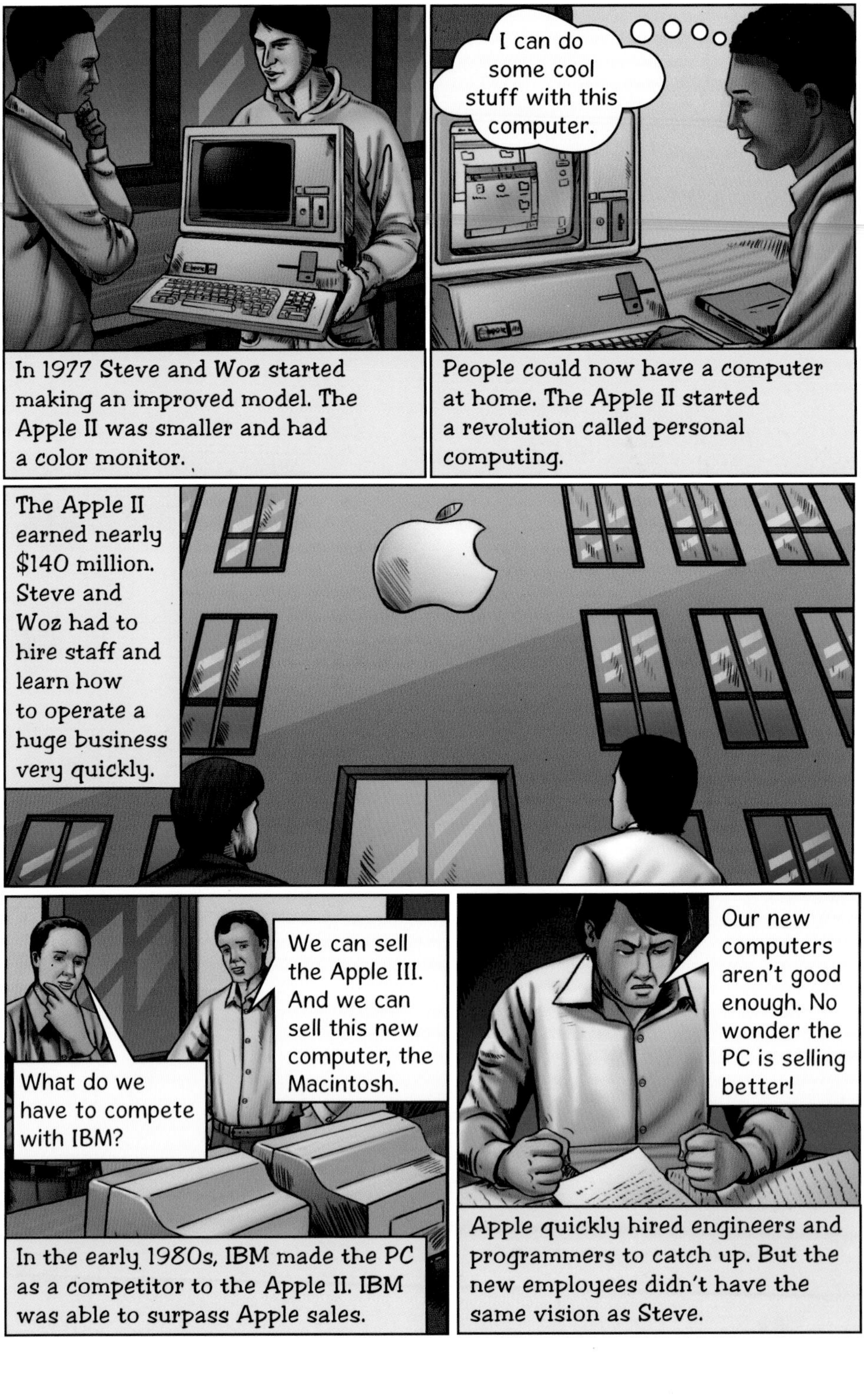
In 1977 Steve and Woz started making an improved model. The Apple II was smaller and had a color monitor.
I can do some cool stuff with this computer.
People could now have a computer at home. The Apple II started a revolution called personal computing.
The Apple II earned nearly $140 million. Steve and Woz had to hire staff and learn how to operate a huge business very quickly.
What do we have to compete with IBM?
We can sell the Apple III. And we can sell this new computer, the Macintosh.
In the early 1980s, IBM made the PC as a competitor to the Apple II. IBM was able to surpass Apple sales.
Our new computers aren't good enough. No wonder the PC is selling better!
Apple quickly hired engineers and programmers to catch up. But the new employees didn't have the same vision as Steve.

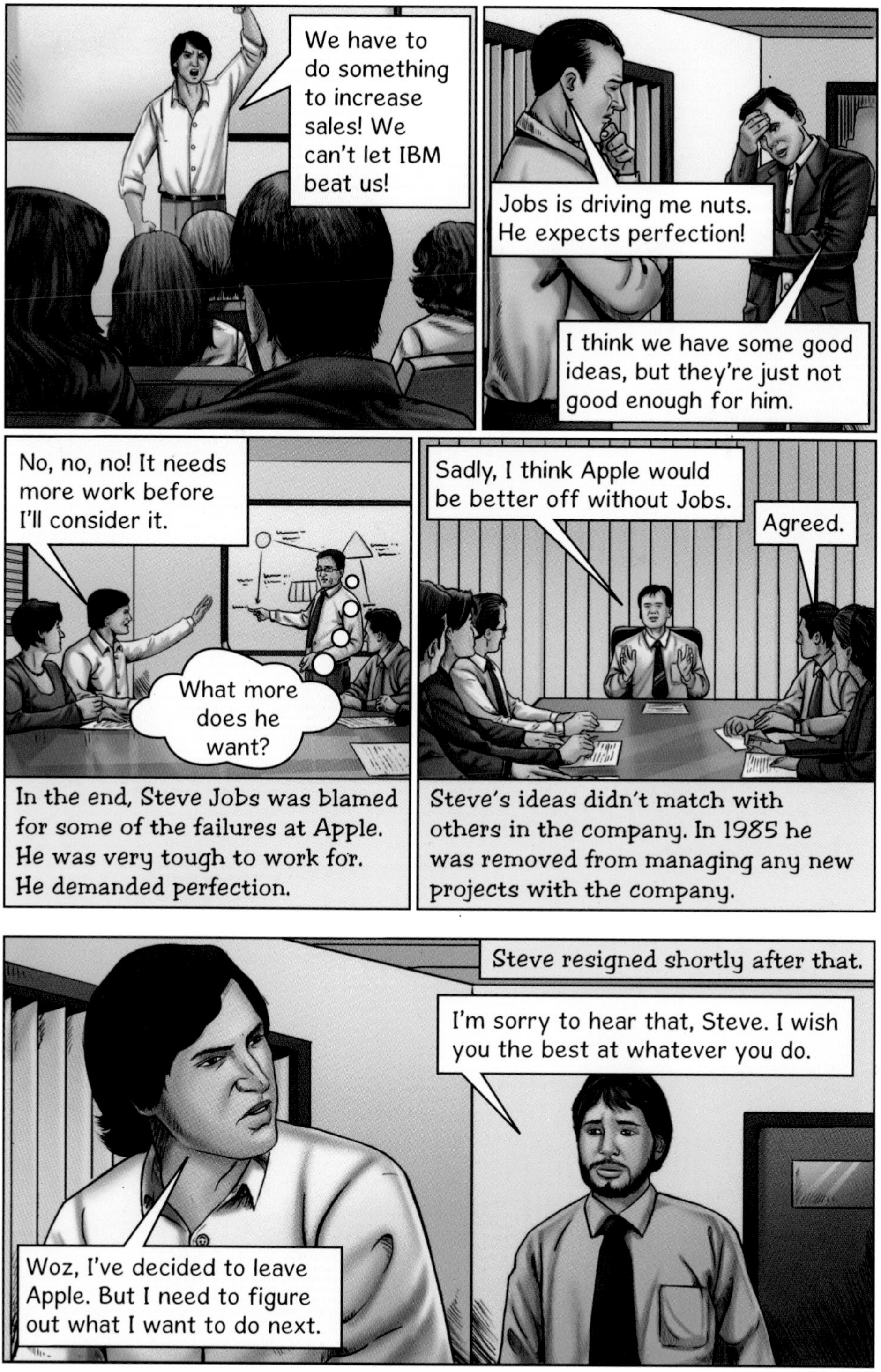
We have to do something to increase sales! We can't let IBM beat us!
Jobs is driving me nuts. He expects perfection!
I think we have some good ideas, but they're just not good enough for him.
No, no, no! It needs more work before I'll consider it.
What more does he want?
In the end, Steve Jobs was blamed for some of the failures at Apple. He was very tough to work for. He demanded perfection.
Sadly, I think Apple would be better off without Jobs.
Agreed.
Steve's ideas didn't match with others in the company. In 1985 he was removed from managing any new projects with the company.
Steve resigned shortly after that.
I'm sorry to hear that, Steve. I wish you the best at whatever you do.
Woz, I've decided to leave Apple. But I need to figure out what I want to do next.

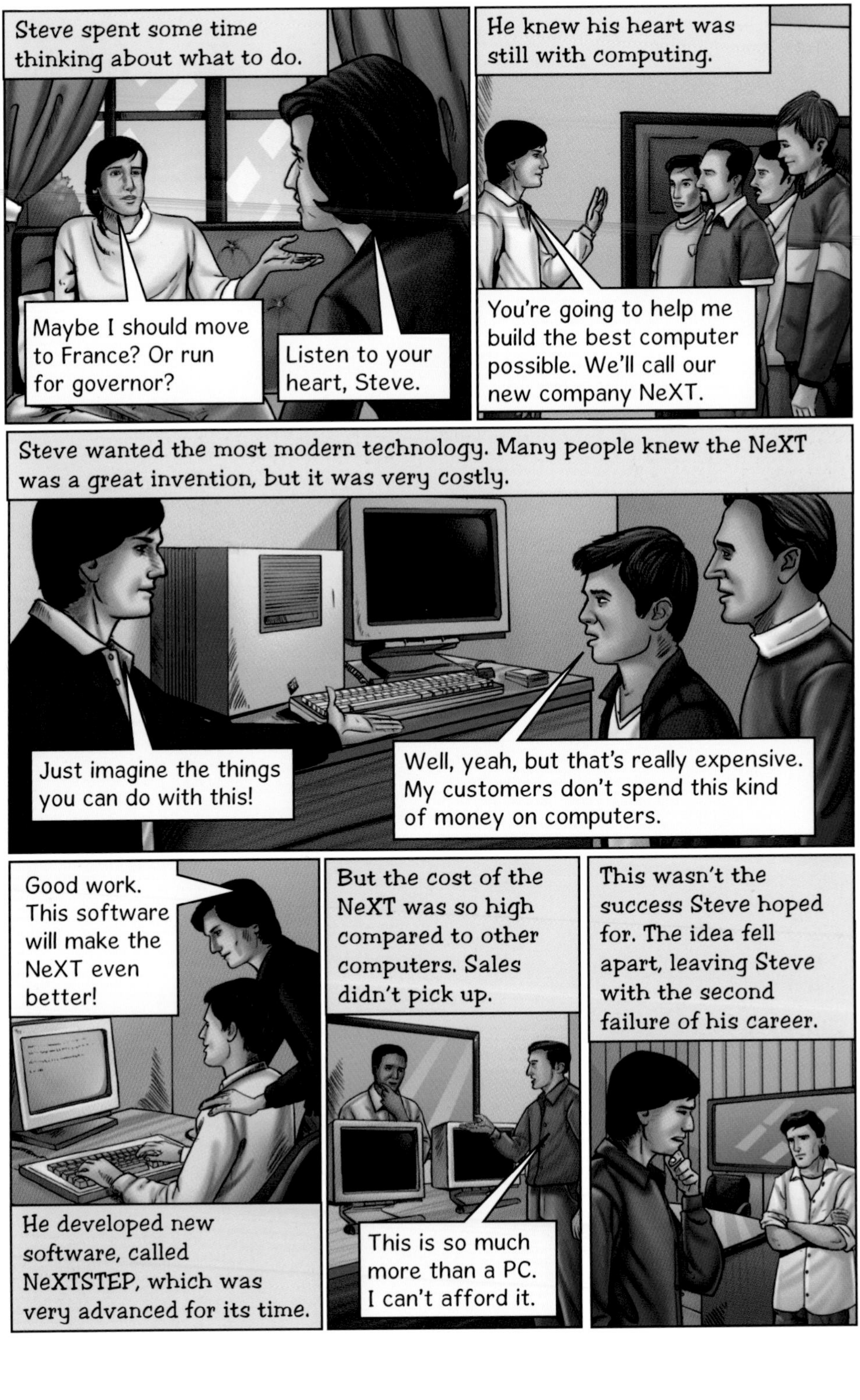
Steve spent some time thinking about what to do.
Maybe I should move to France? Or run for governor?
Listen to your heart, Steve.
He knew his heart was still with computing.
You're going to help me build the best computer possible. We'll call our new company NeXT.
Steve wanted the most modern technology. Many people knew the NeXT was a great invention, but it was very costly.
Just imagine the things you can do with this!
Well, yeah, but that's really expensive. My customers don't spend this kind of money on computers.
Good work. This software will make the NeXT even better!
He developed new software, called NeXTSTEP, which was very advanced for its time.
But the cost of the NeXT was so high compared to other computers. Sales didn't pick up.
This is so much more than a PC. I can't afford it.
This wasn't the success Steve hoped for. The idea fell apart, leaving Steve with the second failure of his career.

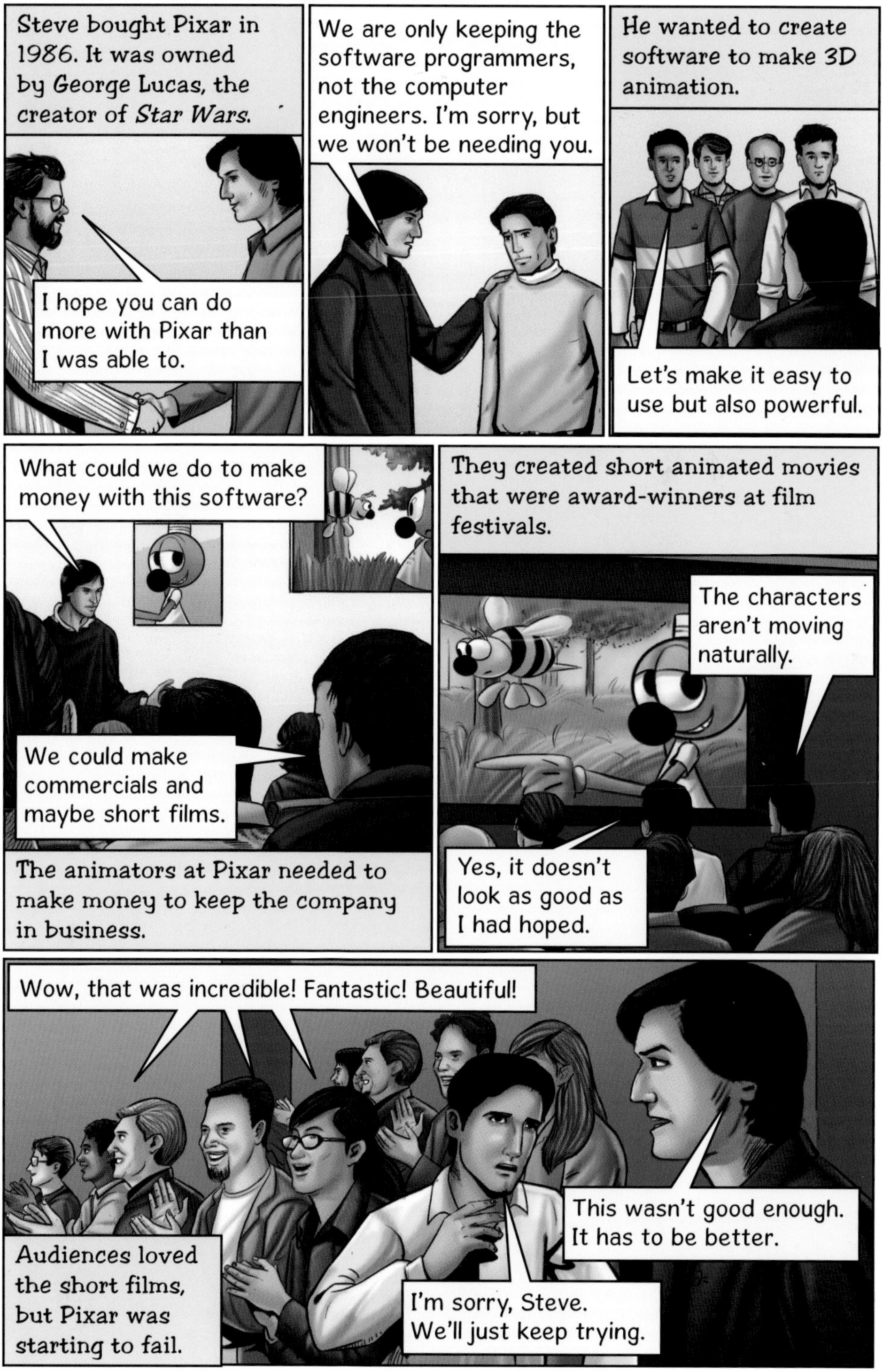
Steve bought Pixar in 1986. It was owned by George Lucas, the creator of *Star Wars*.
I hope you can do more with Pixar than I was able to.
We are only keeping the software programmers, not the computer engineers. I'm sorry, but we won't be needing you.
He wanted to create software to make 3D animation.
Let's make it easy to use but also powerful.
What could we do to make money with this software?
We could make commercials and maybe short films.
The animators at Pixar needed to make money to keep the company in business.
They created short animated movies that were award-winners at film festivals.
The characters aren't moving naturally.
Yes, it doesn't look as good as I had hoped.
Wow, that was incredible! Fantastic! Beautiful!
This wasn't good enough. It has to be better.
Audiences loved the short films, but Pixar was starting to fail.
I'm sorry, Steve. We'll just keep trying.

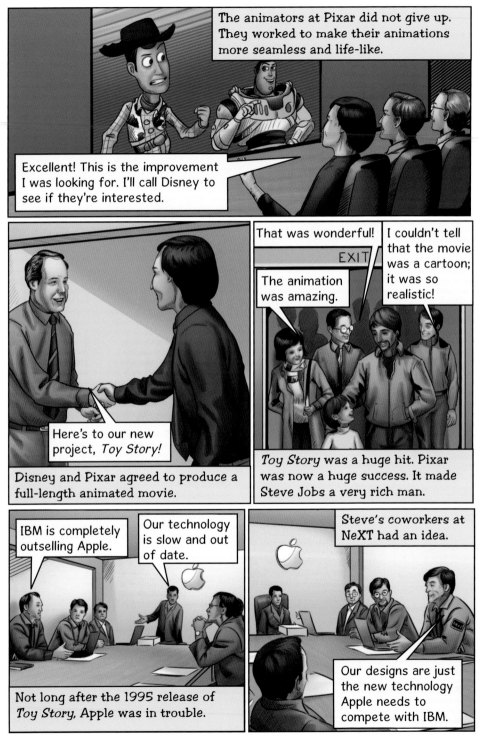

The animators at Pixar did not give up. They worked to make their animations more seamless and life-like.

Excellent! This is the improvement I was looking for. I'll call Disney to see if they're interested.

Here's to our new project, *Toy Story!*

Disney and Pixar agreed to produce a full-length animated movie.

That was wonderful!

EXIT

The animation was amazing.

I couldn't tell that the movie was a cartoon; it was so realistic!

Toy Story was a huge hit. Pixar was now a huge success. It made Steve Jobs a very rich man.

IBM is completely outselling Apple.

Our technology is slow and out of date.

Not long after the 1995 release of *Toy Story*, Apple was in trouble.

Steve's coworkers at NeXT had an idea.

Our designs are just the new technology Apple needs to compete with IBM.

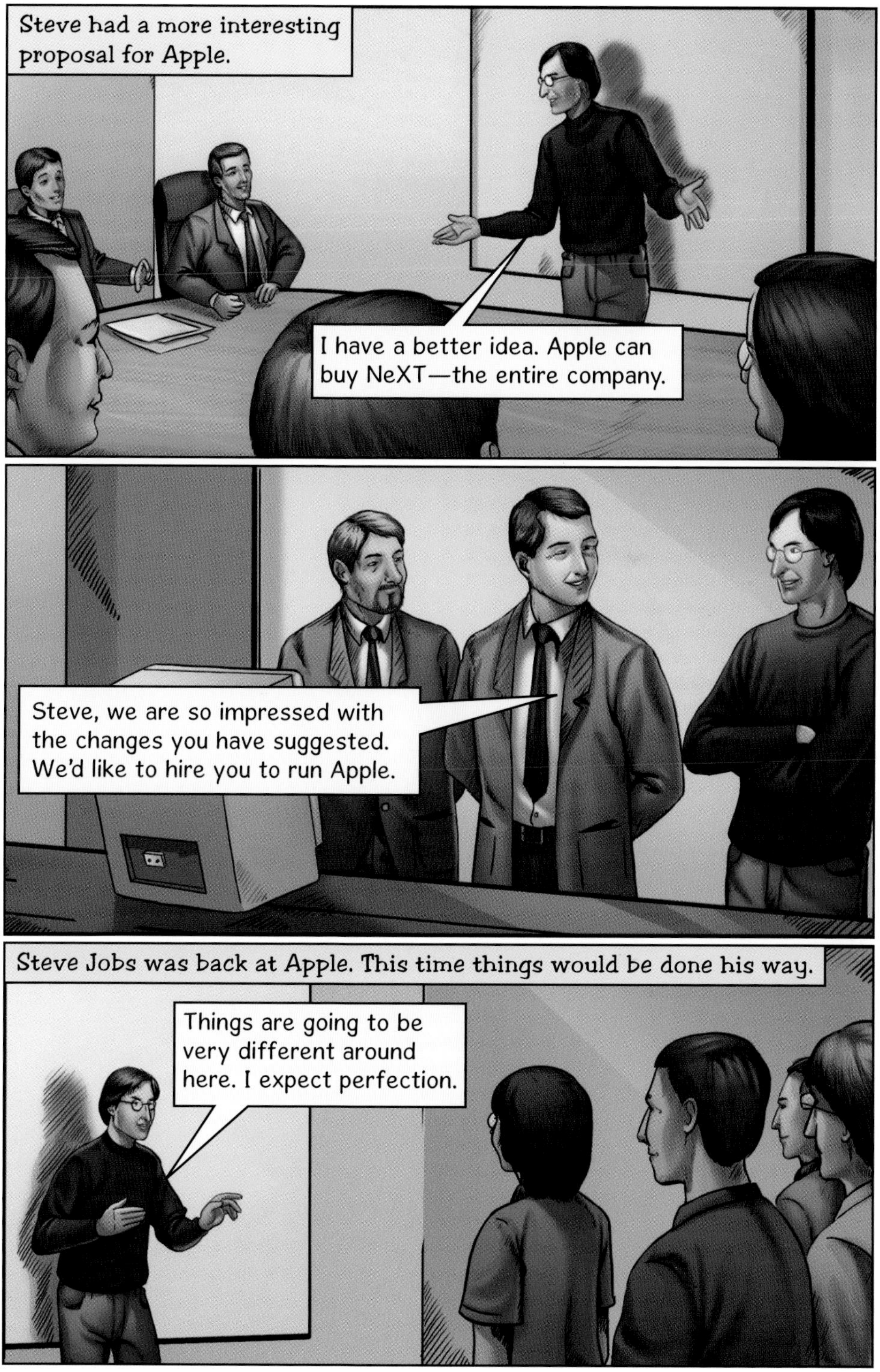
Steve had a more interesting proposal for Apple.
I have a better idea. Apple can buy NeXT—the entire company.
Steve, we are so impressed with the changes you have suggested. We'd like to hire you to run Apple.
Steve Jobs was back at Apple. This time things would be done his way.
Things are going to be very different around here. I expect perfection.

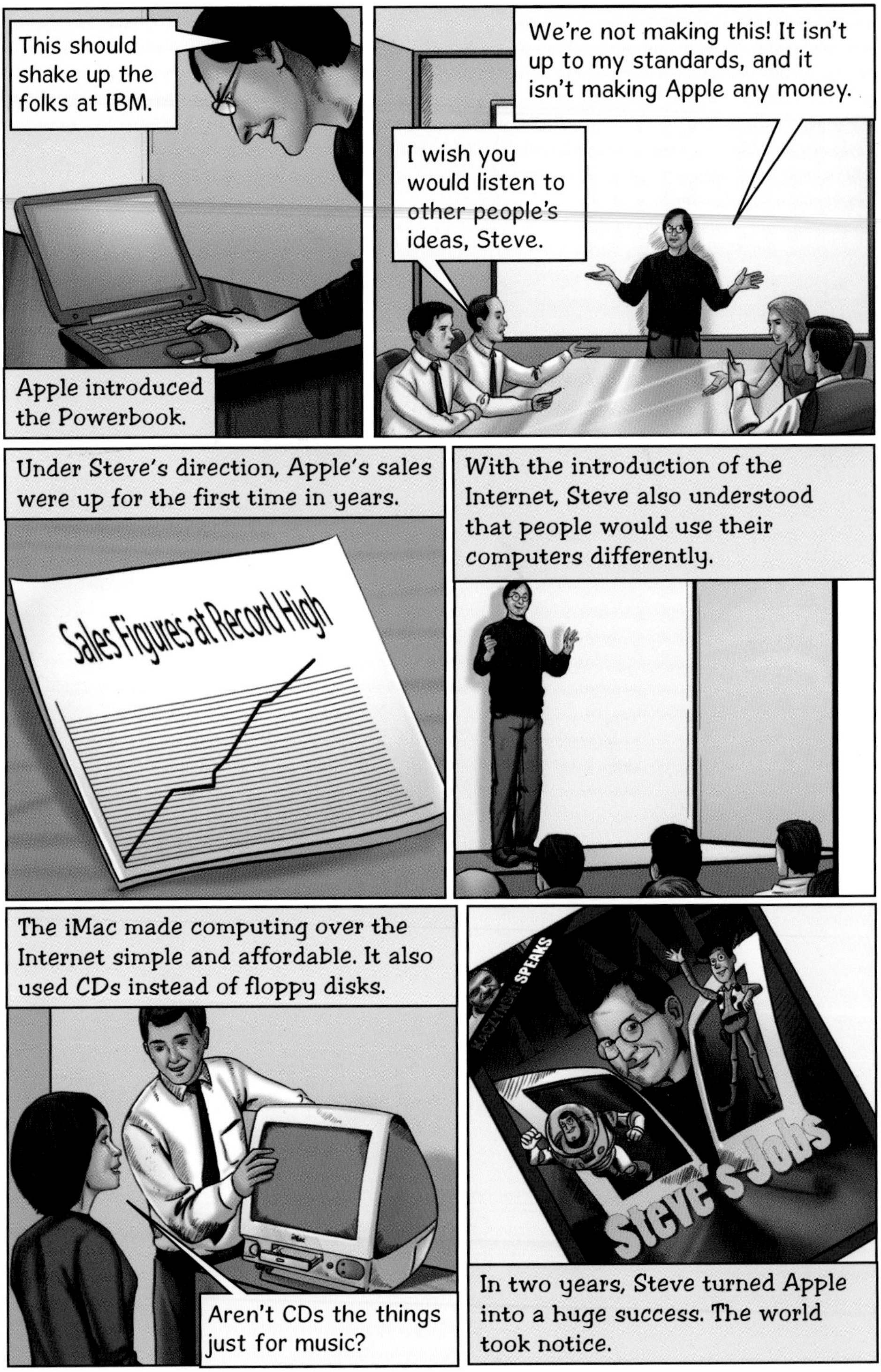
This should shake up the folks at IBM.
Apple introduced the Powerbook.
We're not making this! It isn't up to my standards, and it isn't making Apple any money.
I wish you would listen to other people's ideas, Steve.
Under Steve's direction, Apple's sales were up for the first time in years.
Sales Figures at Record High
With the introduction of the Internet, Steve also understood that people would use their computers differently.
The iMac made computing over the Internet simple and affordable. It also used CDs instead of floppy disks.
Aren't CDs the things just for music?
SPEAKS
Steve's Jobs
In two years, Steve turned Apple into a huge success. The world took notice.

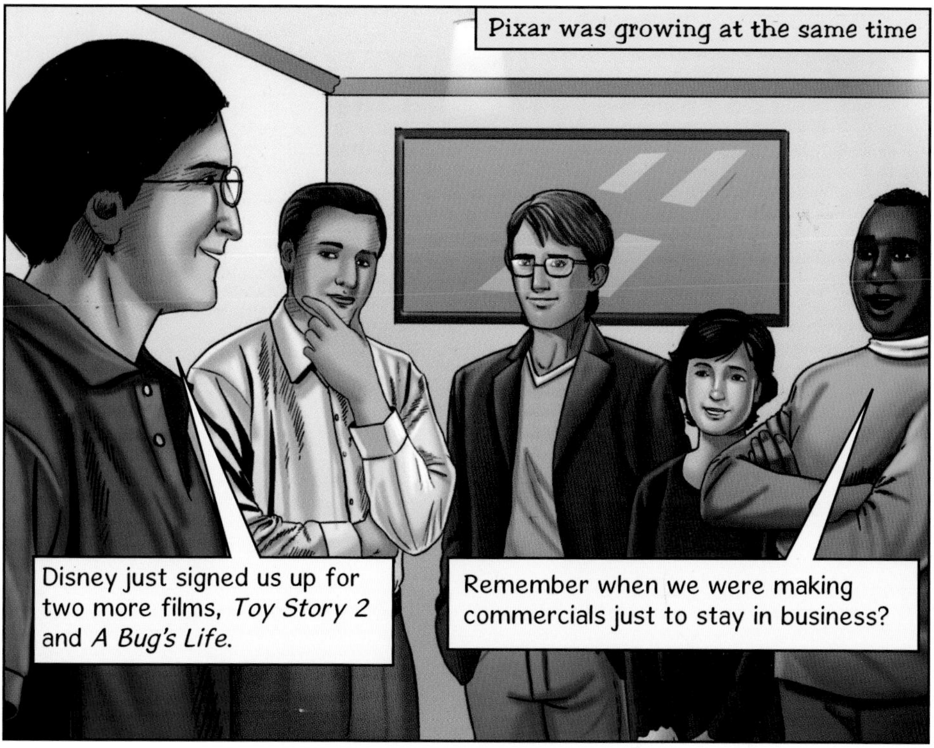
Pixar was growing at the same time
Disney just signed us up for two more films, *Toy Story 2* and *A Bug's Life*.
Remember when we were making commercials just to stay in business?

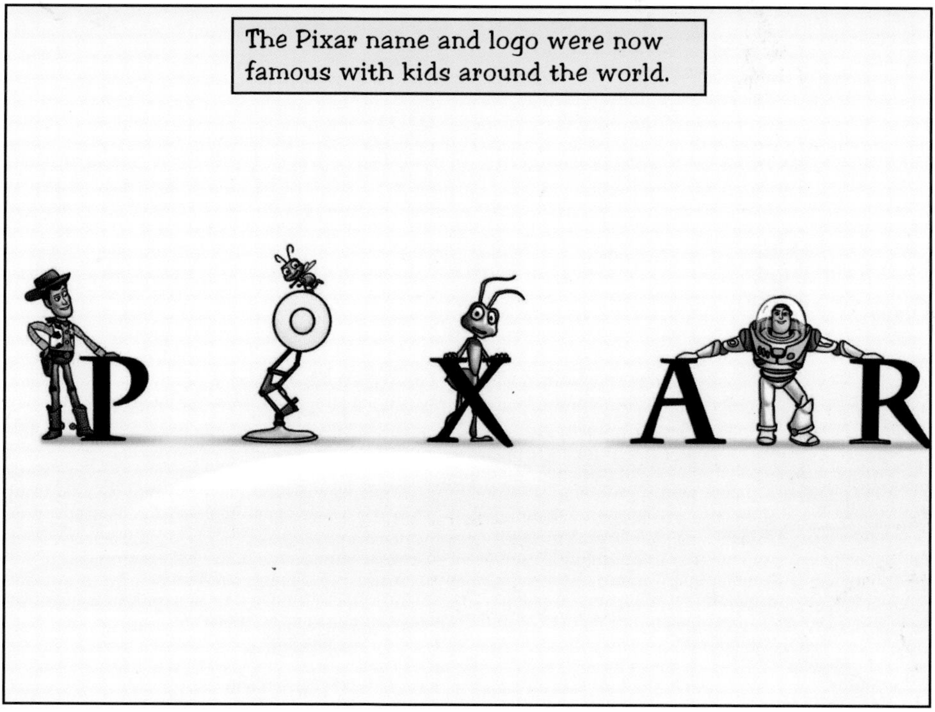
The Pixar name and logo were now famous with kids around the world.
PIXAR

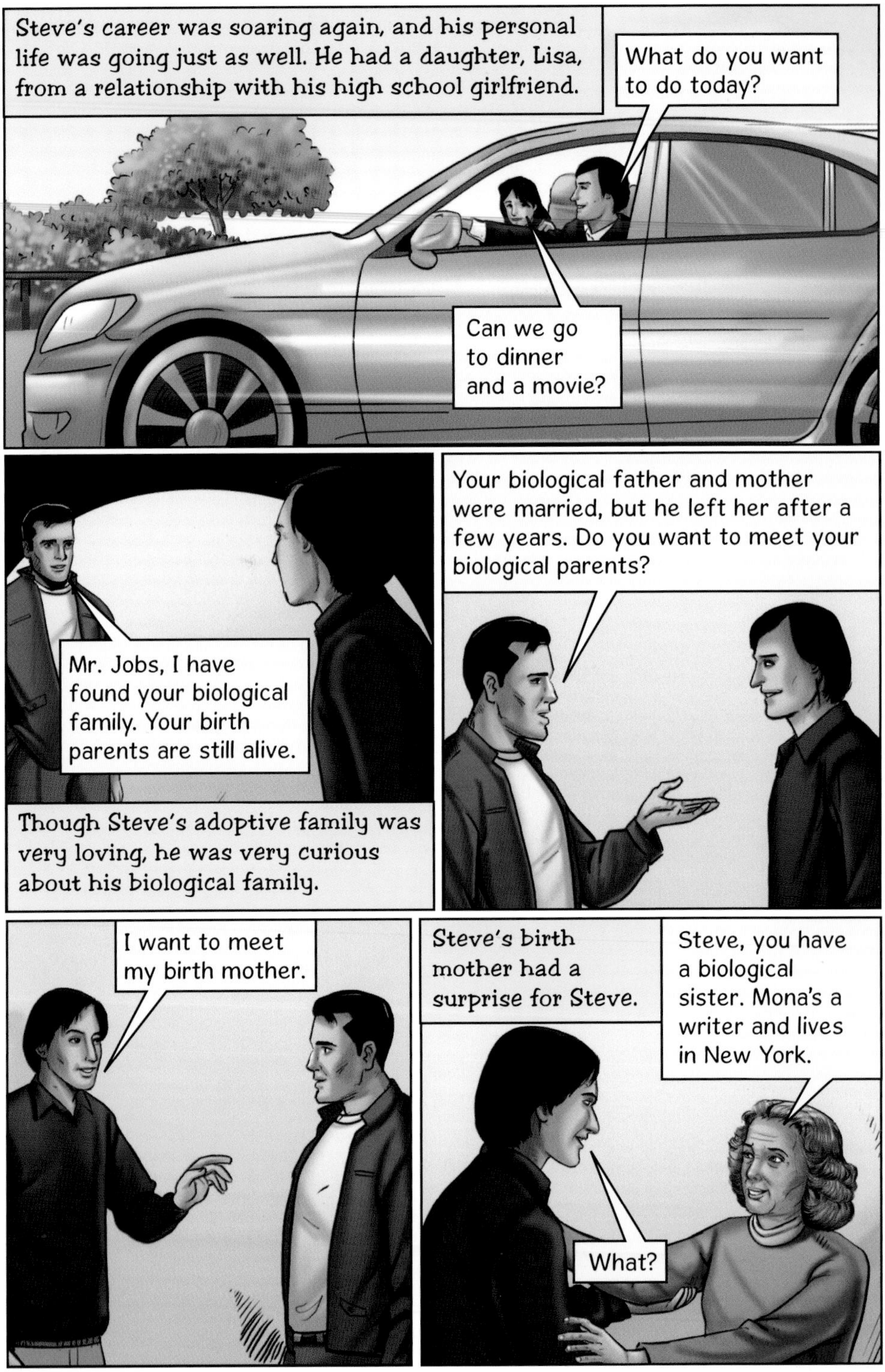
Steve's career was soaring again, and his personal life was going just as well. He had a daughter, Lisa, from a relationship with his high school girlfriend.
What do you want to do today?
Can we go to dinner and a movie?
Mr. Jobs, I have found your biological family. Your birth parents are still alive.
Though Steve's adoptive family was very loving, he was very curious about his biological family.
Your biological father and mother were married, but he left her after a few years. Do you want to meet your biological parents?
I want to meet my birth mother.
Steve's birth mother had a surprise for Steve.
Steve, you have a biological sister. Mona's a writer and lives in New York.
What?

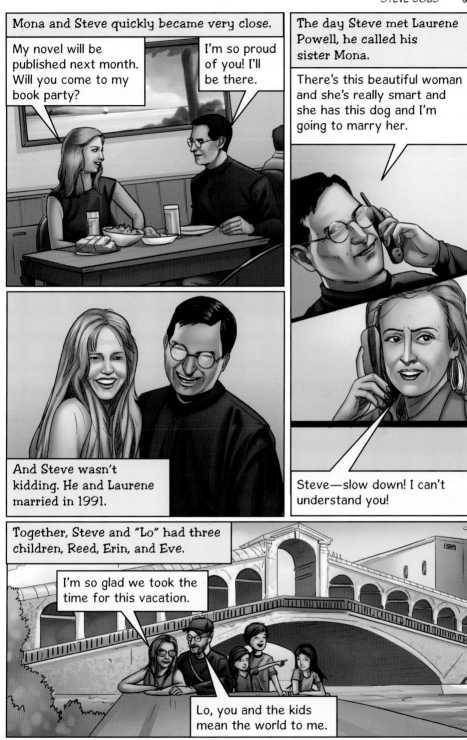

Mona and Steve quickly became very close.

My novel will be published next month. Will you come to my book party?

I'm so proud of you! I'll be there.

And Steve wasn't kidding. He and Laurene married in 1991.

The day Steve met Laurene Powell, he called his sister Mona.

There's this beautiful woman and she's really smart and she has this dog and I'm going to marry her.

Steve—slow down! I can't understand you!

Together, Steve and "Lo" had three children, Reed, Erin, and Eve.

I'm so glad we took the time for this vacation.

Lo, you and the kids mean the world to me.

Apple stayed ahead of how people used technology.

People use the Internet for more than just e-mail. Kids are uploading and downloading illegal copies of music for each other all the time.

Why don't we make a system where downloading music is legal? We can call it ... iTunes!

This iPod connects to your computer to download all the music you want. And it holds thousands of songs instead of the ten to twelve a CD can hold.

The iPod was an instant hit.

Do people with PCs have to buy an Apple computer to get the iPod to work?

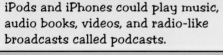

No! We will have a version of the iPod that will work with PCs by next year.

iPods and iPhones could play music, audio books, videos, and radio-like broadcasts called podcasts.

These new releases were in such high demand that people would camp outside of stores to be the first to get the new Apple release.

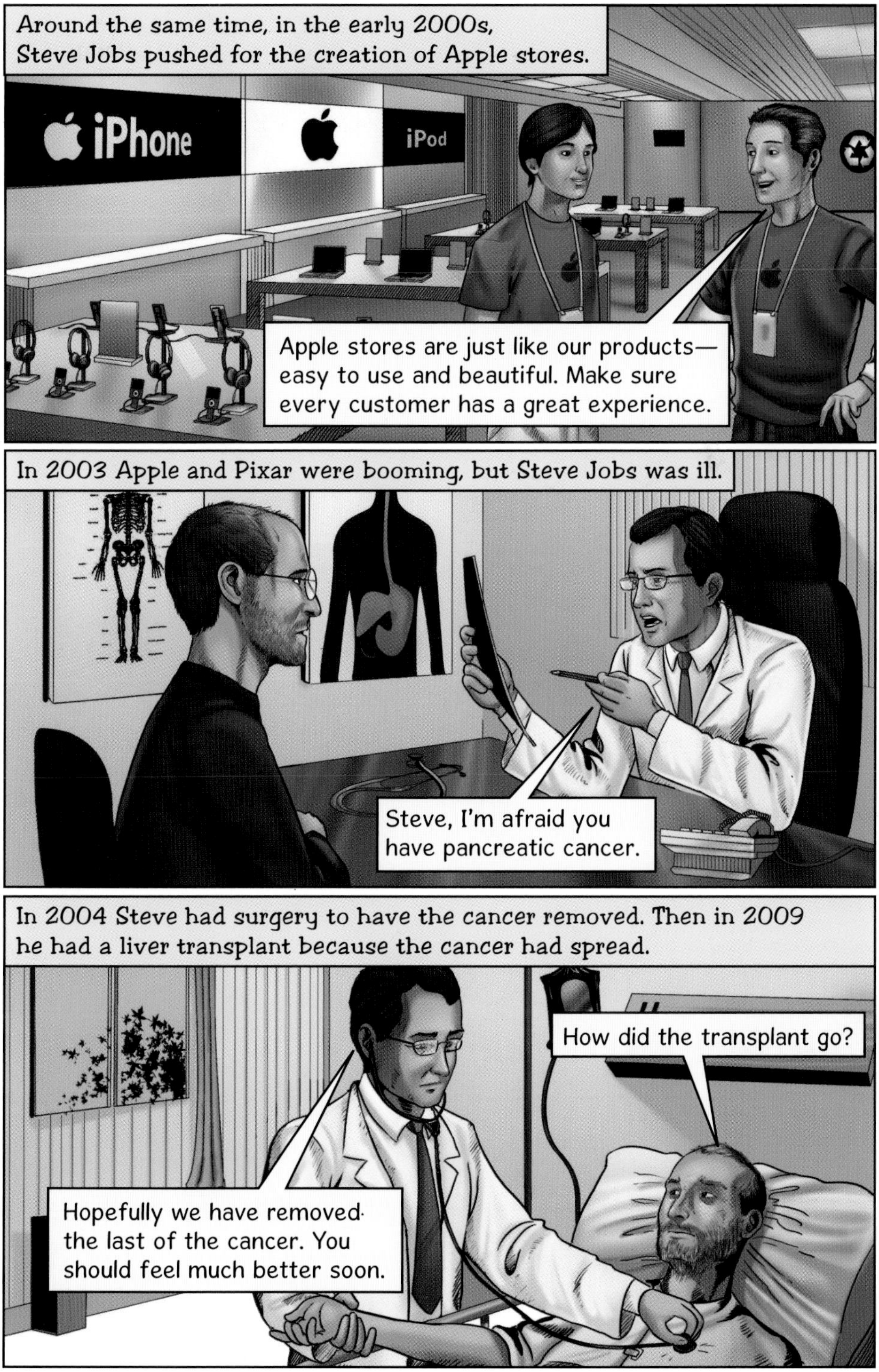
Around the same time, in the early 2000s, Steve Jobs pushed for the creation of Apple stores.
iPhone
iPod
Apple stores are just like our products—easy to use and beautiful. Make sure every customer has a great experience.
In 2003 Apple and Pixar were booming, but Steve Jobs was ill.
Steve, I'm afraid you have pancreatic cancer.
In 2004 Steve had surgery to have the cancer removed. Then in 2009 he had a liver transplant because the cancer had spread.
How did the transplant go?
Hopefully we have removed the last of the cancer. You should feel much better soon.

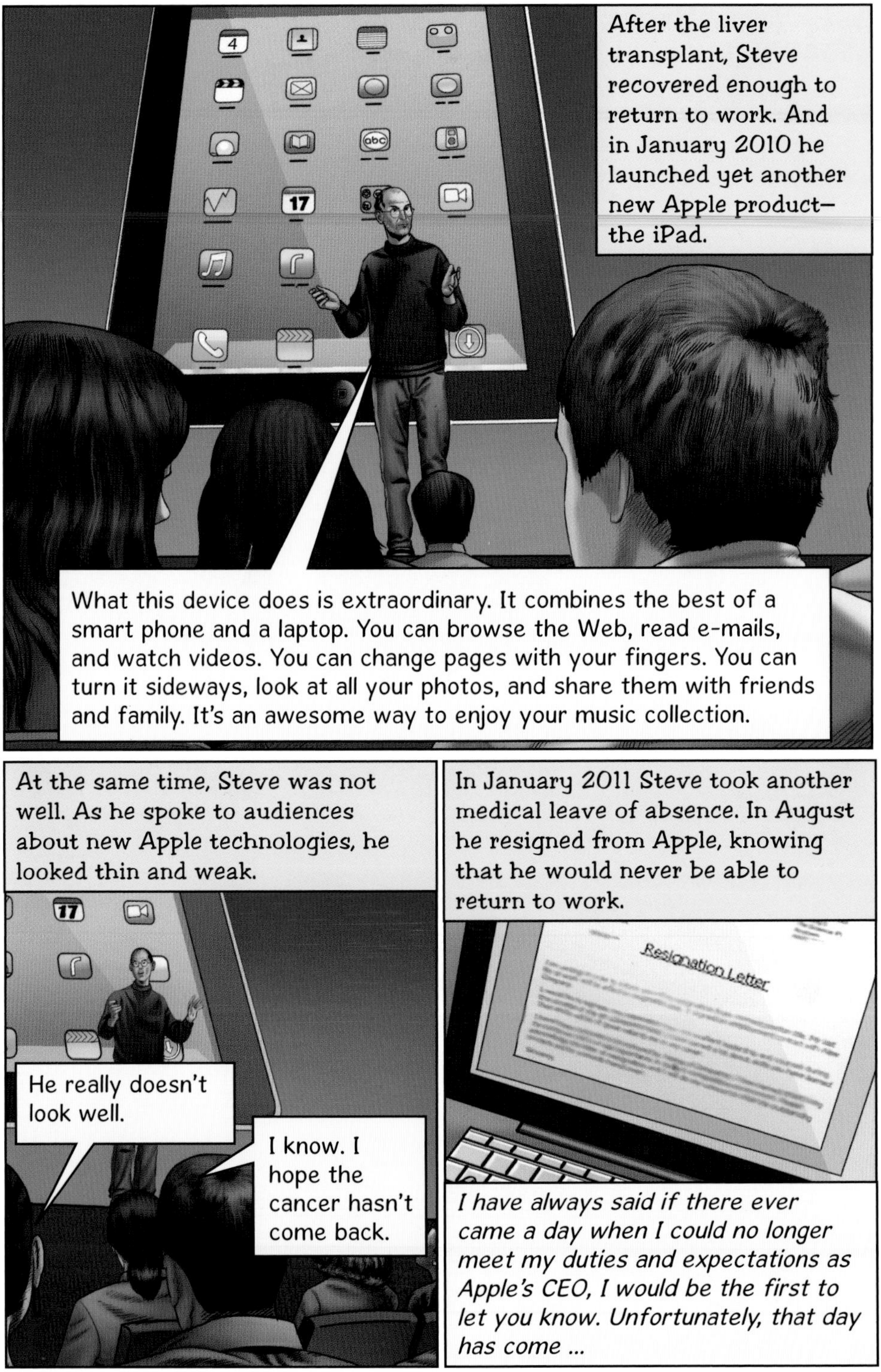
After the liver transplant, Steve recovered enough to return to work. And in January 2010 he launched yet another new Apple product—the iPad.
What this device does is extraordinary. It combines the best of a smart phone and a laptop. You can browse the Web, read e-mails, and watch videos. You can change pages with your fingers. You can turn it sideways, look at all your photos, and share them with friends and family. It's an awesome way to enjoy your music collection.
At the same time, Steve was not well. As he spoke to audiences about new Apple technologies, he looked thin and weak.
He really doesn't look well.
I know. I hope the cancer hasn't come back.
In January 2011 Steve took another medical leave of absence. In August he resigned from Apple, knowing that he would never be able to return to work.
Resignation Letter
I have always said if there ever came a day when I could no longer meet my duties and expectations as Apple's CEO, I would be the first to let you know. Unfortunately, that day has come ...

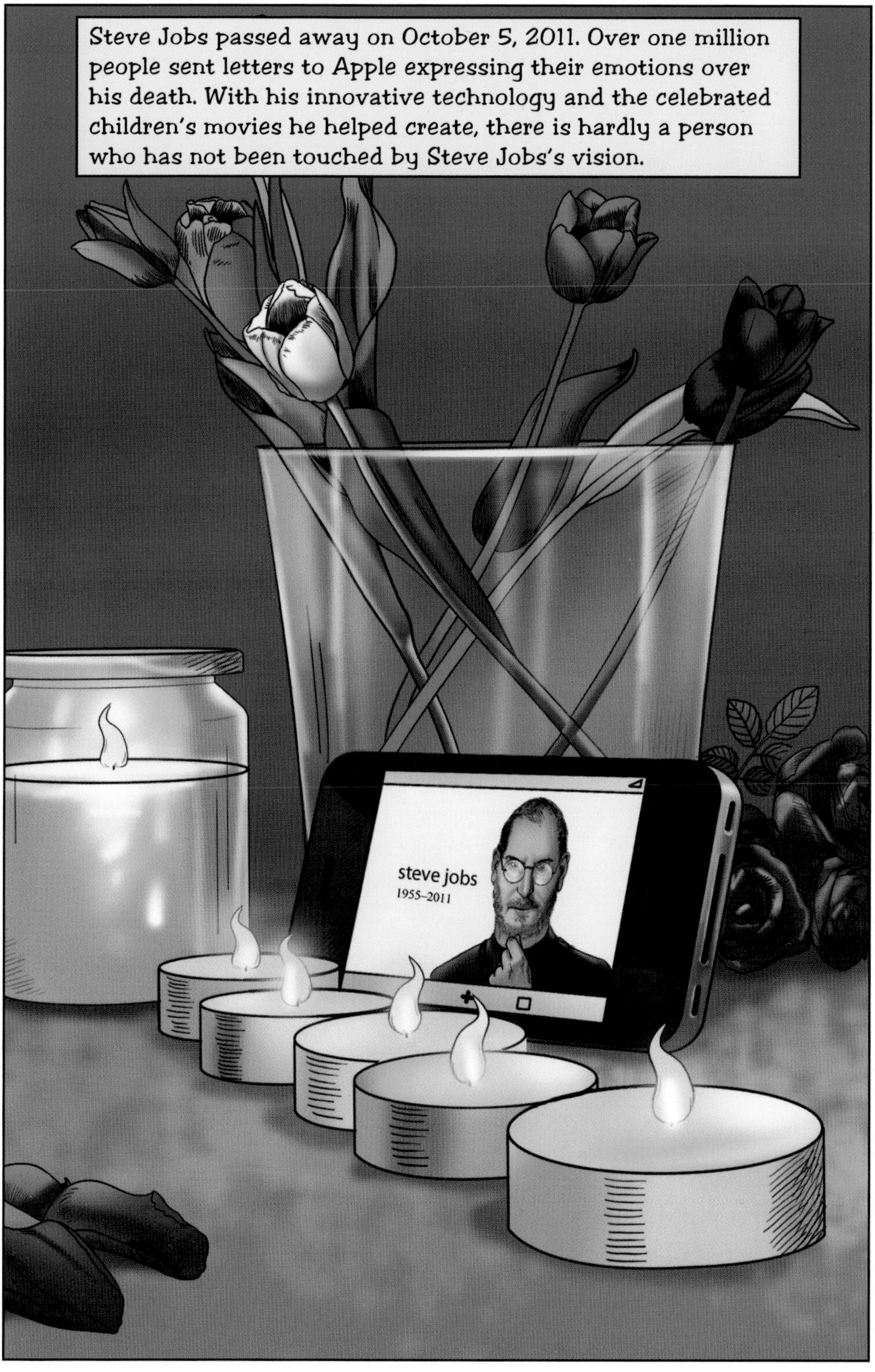
Steve Jobs passed away on October 5, 2011. Over one million people sent letters to Apple expressing their emotions over his death. With his innovative technology and the celebrated children's movies he helped create, there is hardly a person who has not been touched by Steve Jobs's vision.
steve jobs
1955–2011

JB JOBS STE

Steve Jobs.

ELK